Robyn Cairns

Horizon

Horizon
ISBN 978 1 76109 473 6
Copyright © text Robyn Cairns 2023
Cover image: Robyn Cairns

First published 2023 by
GINNINDERRA PRESS
PO Box 3461 Port Adelaide 5015
www.ginninderrapress.com.au

For Ewan and Judy
who were so very resilient
throughout Victoria's six lockdowns
during the global Covid-19 pandemic
between 2020 and 2021

Thank you to our wonderful healthcare workers

canopy
the rest of the world
disappears

sunday meditation
one raindrop
joins another

first cosmos
the beautiful world
of my backyard

hibiscus down the old laneway
a long time lost
in this world

twenty-twenty
a new member
of the cloud-watching club

barefoot
across night grass
the joy of cricket song

backyard serenade
fairy wrens
without aeroplanes

amidst city smoke haze
I pull over
for a magnolia

working from home
I shift my chair
into a sunbeam

barely visible
moon scrapes
the old garage

emerging to a changed Earth cicada

first night in the soil
little lettuce seedlings
feel the moon

up late
the whispers
of my indoor plants

nowhere to go
the repeated pattern
of mum's old cardigan

after midnight
mapping a new garden
in my mind

blue-wrapped sky
one little bird
writes a poem

wandering feathers
soft fragments of me
in the sky

late autumn swim
a cormorant bobs up
beside me

against a backdrop
of industry
soft shapes of waterbirds

crepuscular light
a long silhouette
of suburbia

lips on a pricky pear a sharp left turn

lockdown
the time I watched
a whole rose open

along the garage gutter
a blackbird collecting
raindrops

strange days
rain falling
on blank pages

written all over
my mental health care plan
flight and music of birds

sunday night
the scent
of an open book

nearly midnight
an empty train
full of moonlight

fading afternoon
creating a sculpture
in the dish rack

beer-soaked carpets
the last gig
plays on

late night
following the moon
down the hallway

Demolition Street

Demolition guys are demolishing. Demolished another heritage Hansen weatherboard today. The apple green weatherboard went down today. Voice louder than bulldozers as I tried to save a pair of blue birds stained glassed into the sun for the last eighty years. Bulldozers devoured the whole house in a few rapid heartbeats. Razed flat from Dempster Street. Even the '45 penny under green linoleum was taken. My heart went down today. No Hills hoist spinning in summer sun. No bluebirds flying into sunrise.

    searching for blue glass in a heart of rubble

icy air
the warm crunch
of a chiko roll

broken windows
pigeons fill
a lonely warehouse

winter breath
a poem
on the car window

winter moon
fills the yard
tuning an old radio

suburban relics
a letter box
in bloom

early evening
the last songbirds
sing into my veins

global heartache
the collective grief
of strangers

midnight
loading thoughts
onto a passing train

wild weather
daffodils kiss
the ground

filtered light
my son and I
read the trees together

shoreline walks
the blues and blues
of bottle tops

wild moon grasslands
eastern barred bandicoots
back from the brink

inhaling jasmine inhaling sun

a small hand
trickles seeds
into spring soil
do we all dream
of sunflowers?

children buzzing
about the garden
sweet peas

Cherry lake
spills into the creek
six spoonbills
sieving the edge
of the overflow

crossing off
days in ISO
Clarissa sends
an egret
from her phone

two-hundredth day in lockdown googling blowflies

waiting for sunset
a small fairy wren
and then another
hop across the back fence
as beautiful as that

nightfall
watching a wattlebird
shimmy a wire

Little Desert National Park   April 2021

mallee scrub
a billow of dust
behind an emu

white sand tracks –
desert banksias aglow
with sunrise

Little Desert Track -
rising from a conifer
a plume of honeyeaters

The Last Two Weeks

Andy my hairdresser
Lost her cat Lola in Lockdown 4
On Matthews Hill
In Sunshine

Lola was wearing
Her green collar and brass bell

I printed her missing poster
On my brain
Andy crept through the dead quiet streets
When all were asleep
Calling   L o l a   on repeat
This lockdown wasn't like the others
No teddy bears in windows
Or rainbows on the street
No baking cinnamon scrolls
Just a finger up at Scomo
Who hadn't vaccinated
Our elderly or ambos
Never will be…my PM
and the rain was relentless
Floods and storms
              and damage and sadness
and Lola she's gone missing
it's been a winter blues
two weeks

nearly spring
one daffodil
becomes a row

resting place
the rain within
a rose whorl

carrying afternoon sun
tree to tree
wattlebird

Stage 4 Lockdown Melbourne – For Jo

Google Meet me on the sunny side
of curfew in a dream of curlews
in flight across an electric blue
pollution-free solar-powered sky
our cars go nowhere
in this emission free city
star filled southern cross night skies
replace our neon pulsing nights
a message woven by a spider
glistening in sun
no more WebEx
meet me by the seashore
free of plastic pieces
celebrating this new age love
of urban environment
everybody noticing nature
sprouting from cracks in footpaths
spilling over corrugated fences
singing from trees -
feet in soft Altona sand
reading each other's masked smiles
side by side and silent
too worn for words
watching frilled bay waves
creep towards longing toes

the sound of waves
soundwaves
waves of sound
waves from the shore
shoreline
birds line the shore
sure lines

magic carpet magnolia high

spilling into twilight every brushstroke

sixth lockdown pulling creativity from the clouds

Opening from Lockdown 6

folding her wings
wondering
does a butterfly feel
the capture of breath
or the touch of symmetry?
tracing her fluttering flight path
feeling safe
inside a sunny suburban yard
stretching out with our dog
along strips of sun, I sigh
content away from queues and crowds
unmasked faces
crawling traffic
and price hikes
soft grass under bare feet

heart becoming open sky a blue-winged parrot

dusk splash
in our bird bath
specs of goldfinch gold

clear city night
a ring-tailed possum
star gazing

december morning
in every room
fairy wrens

first sweep
of my paddle blade
the tilt of a heron

rural backroads
every direction
a sea of stars

migration flyways
of the future
godwits go interstellar

Tarra-Bulga

Lyrebird Ridge Track. Two birders wrapped in binoculars like me. We stop to share smiles and wish lists. Pilot birds, pink robins, and elusive lyrebirds. Tips are exchanged and I tuck Toora in my back pocket. Swinging across the Tarra Bulga trestle bridge through towering tree ferns I become cool temperate forest. My skin is moss. I am printed in the lace shadows of fern fronds. This forest is where magic is born I believe. Car windows down for mountain ash and forest birds. Winding alongside Tarra River until curved roads become straight. Straight roads lead to Port Albert. Rodondo cottages. I cook Swiss brown mushrooms and too much cauliflower and cheese. Port Albert birdsong through the open sash windows.

> forest bathing far away from a flooded city

summer pier
slowing my stride
across the sea

monday in Port Albert
street pines wrapped
in Xmas bows

Toora bird hide
strangers share
a common love

letting go opening arms to the wild sea

barely a whimbrel the breathing roots of mangroves

Down the Bird Line

One Hudsonian whimbrel has turned up in Toora. The birders have been passing it on. Inside Toora bird hide huddled with scopes and binoculars and all birding paraphernalia. Focus my fogged-up bargain binoculars. Anticipation builds. A slight breeze travels through the hide. We hope together inside this quiet place full of strangers who love birds. Scanning amongst the fifty-plus eastern curlews and one hundred bar tailed godwits. The lone Hudsonian whimbrel eludes but everything along the shoreline I see is happiness.

    dreamers collective a hopeful future for birds

crescent moon the cry of an eastern curlew

Corner Inlet

turn the worn wood latches
hook up the chains
slots of blue sky
inside long frames
where mangroves sprawl
across mudflats
and crabs click the air
in the bird hide
alone and content I watch
eastern curlews shift
from statuesque stillness
to preen, roam and probe the shoreline
happiness is the arc
of an eastern curlew's bill
over and over and over

saluting the sun in unison with a blackbird

hanging washing
in the night
pockets of cricket song

august afternoon
a flock of ibis
draft poetry

on vivid
winter grass
I count ten fairy wrens

blurred horizon line the pandemic years

Acknowledgements

Poems in this book have appeared in the following publications:
'twenty twenty': *Echidna Tracks*, Australian Haiku, Issue 5
'nowhere to go': *Prune Juice*, Journal of English Senryu and
Related Forms, Issue 35, Senryu and Related Forms
'late autumn swim': *Windfall*, Issue 9, Australian Haiku
'against a backdrop' and 'resting place': *Seashores,
An international journal to share the spirit of haiku*
'two hundredth day' and 'sixth lockdown': *Failed Haiku*,
A journal of English Senryu
'mallee scrub': *Windfall*, Issue 10, Australian Haiku
'saluting the sun' and 'spilling into twilight': *Hedgerow*,
A journal of small poems
'heart becoming open sky' and 'back from the brink':
The Bloō Outlier Journal
'barely a whimbrel': *Whiptail*, journal of the single-line poem,
Issue 2, summoning the sky, February 2022

www.ingramcontent.com/pod-product-compliance
Lightning Source LLC
Chambersburg PA
CBHW070339120526
44590CB00017B/2948